SCORCHED BIRTH

poems

John Curl

Ebook & 2nd edition paperback
Homeward Press, 2026
ISBN: 978-1-7335775-7-1 (E-book, 2026)
ISBN: 978-1-7335775-6-4 (Paperback, 2026)

First edition paperback, Beatitude Press, 2004
ISBN: 0-9759934-3-7

Homeward Press
Berkeley, CA
https://johncurl.net/

SCORCHED BIRTH

THE RAVEN SPOKE ABOUT THE WAR

White-Crested Waves
Babbling Brooks are Caressed
First Robin of Spring
Sparrows Whisper About
Pounding the Southern City

MISTAKEN IDENTITIES

The Harrowing Stench of the Defense
Caught in an Endless Loop
Scattered about the Village Well
The Bounty of Acorns
Green Tree Frogs Sing
Red Squirrels Chase Each Other
A Splurge of Spiked Vervains
Surrounded by Mirrors

KEYS TO THE WAR ROOM

Crows
A Leaf Twirling
Splinters of Mirror
Earthquake Under the Ocean
Marries
The Doll of a Homeless Girl

HOMAGE TO GONZALO GUERRERO

Foreword

Discover the electricity in language, unmask the mind, follow the unbroken spirit through content and conflict in John Curl's latest book Scorched Birth. A Master Poet who uses language in a remarkable, innovative way, he gives us information on contradictions in the evolving state of human consciousness.

The tensile lines of these poems are a strong loom holding the strength of an interwoven theme of Social Justice making deliberate design through the poet's understanding of actions and attitudes.

John Curl shows us the undersides of clouds and cultures but also shows immutable order in chaos. He can, in a single poem, give at least 15 ways of changing personal, social, political darkness, including purification by fire. Though some are seemingly surreal, strange and new, your intellect tells you each line is someone's reality at the core.

Many poets and a wide following of readers have long loved John Curl's work for his content and craftsmanship discovering, as in the prose of Jack Kerouac, the sudden haiku and haiku sequences within the longer work. An example (in John Curl's poem Green Tree Frogs Sing): " ... A swallowtail butterfly flutters past the row of prisoners, hands wired behind their backs... "

Images flash from "broken egg shell" bodies of War dead to "how much light there is in darkness .... " In some poems, the poet asks questions we can believe birds and forests understand.

My personal favorite for sheer love of imagery is ``Green Flowers Drizzle Down."

Through jaguar eyes the poet looks at history, ending his book with a Mayan/Spanish Epic permeated with deep respect for nature, waters, salmon, centuries of passionate life. Throughout the book, his unique lines glisten with gold, coin of words fall from his pages into your hands to become your personal treasure. You find yourself more wealthy and wise than you were before you chose it to read, moved, disturbed, awakened, yet fulfilled, rich with pleasure.

Mary Rudge, author of *Water Planet*

SCORCHED BIRTH

"In an age of information's uprooting of everything, John Curl's *Scorched Birth* creates, through a fusion of data and metaphor, a magical poetry that resonates with classical American (Mayan) simultaneity. This is a book of wonders."

– Jack Hirschman , author of *Front Lines*

JEWELS IN THE RUBBLE

THE TRAGEDY AT THE CORE

Information on what's going on
on the ground is sketchy.
They only show us the bomber's eye view.
Reverberations of shelling bounce off
the mountain sides.
The nervous ladies chatting
about fashionable colors.
A pale thin moon circling the ring.
Misty peaks sink into the
dark surface of the bay.
Light rippling.
While the mountain passes are littered
with decomposing corpses lying
as they died.
No one approaches.
Except a bulldozer driver and six
jumpy soldiers. He dumps
dirt on top of the pile. Yet
in the midst we try
to lead decent lives, create a
just society, even love and try to
purify our human soul. Maybe
we have to just accept the
contradictions. Nearby,
a gray wolf with frightened eyes
dashes across a moonlit stream.

MUTED SHADES OF BROWN

walk along the park at night,
past the small fountain in the school yard where
women once washed clothes.
Moonlight filters through foliage
past the distant barking
of a beaten dog.
Later that night
multi-colored jasper and the essence
of trees were reduced to eating
bark and leaves,
twenty six homes were burned,
police put an automatic rifle to her cheek,
a stream of battered cars crawled
to the outskirts of town where
hundreds of drunk soldiers
blocked the road. The civic center,
an ancient market, now
no longer exists.
An old carpet, frayed along
the path to the door.
Tropical fish in deep pools in
the eyes of Emiliano Zapata.
Strange rhythms beat on a clay drum.
Sky and earth become one.

THE CLOUDS' UNDERSIDES

were dark and ragged while
their tops shined and billowed
above the bare hills, almost
devoid of vegetation while
not far away, in the grass by
a whispering stream at the
very spot where wilderness
holds back civilization,
the ruins of an ancient temple
wince from shrapnel wounds.
The state of human consciousness in
our darkest age.
Vehicles scatter in charred twisted
heaps. Unsafe to go outside.
They refuse to identify the bodies.
A small girl with a redhaired rag doll,
left for dead, at nightfall crawls away.
Is this our purification by fire?

OUR LIVES ON A SUMMER BREEZE

we have nothing but our hands.
Some fifty thousand refugees
stream out, the report states,
independently confirmed.
Rocket-propelled grenades punch
holes in all the barn roofs,
looting rampages along main street,
no food or medicine getting through,
she picks up the baby,
cluster bomb explodes,
you prick yourself on a thorn:
your lover is lying to you
one drop of blood sits on your fingertip.
a huge antlered stag silouettes for an instant
against the night sky.
Rebuilding shattered dreams.

THE SUN ROSE ON A FOGGY

rain-soaked rags in the gutter
chalk drawings of disturbed children
living in abandoned houses
blackened roof shingles scattered across
floors inlaid with precious stone
piles of broken toys sinking
into moist earth at the bottom of the pit
charred dismembered dreams lying where they
died
mass graves strewn with
rotting hearts and burnt minds
roof beams lying across the kitchen table
their village still off limits
until its goals are acheived
the ten American corporations
which own the media
ordered them to leave or be shot
when she realized that she had to live bravely
and the sun shines darkness too

SHEET METAL FLAPS IN THE BREEZE

jets strafe the country road
packed with the day's refugees
fireballs over the vegetable market
a premature greenness haunts the fields
blind men wash the streets
magpies wing above the ruins
sprouts still encircle the stump
the eldest would have been eight years old
she haunted recesses of his mind
all those wasted years

nothing at the scene evidenced
a military target

ALL OF OUR MEN ARE GONE

a rain of frogs
broken pitcher
the point at which hope is extinguished
muffled explosions echo from the mountain sides
a cousin shot dead
he thinks they are in hiding
endless chorus of loss
nestled in the folds of the valley
the old thatched roof
lumps of black earth in plowed fields
a clean bare room
walking along the empty shore
an early spring rain
girl who dreams great dreams

VEIL OF MIST AROUND THE SUN

movement of light through the leaves
her glove in his hand
the pool surrounded by willows, lilacs, gladioli,
irises
city burning for the fifty-fifth day
tourists replaced by terrorists
launching a major new offensive
the vast majority out all night in rain
impossible to confirm casualty figures
as air raid sirens sounded again at mid-morning
along with his two sons
intelligence on the ground is sketchy
she has the look of a madwoman
a starry night with cypresses
I wish you could fill your lungs with it

A FEW OLD MEN HAVE FOUND SHELTER IN THE BASEMENT

What kind of love did I feel
ten days hiding in the woods
smoldering tractors and trailers
spinal fractures, every degree burns
allowed to return to the rubble of my home
the roof of the freight depot scattered on the sidewalk
many crows circling about
the trail along the inlet from the sea
street lamps reflected in puddles
view from the school window
woman beside a cradle
an abundant growth of green moss

TOWERS SILHOUETTE AGAINST THE SKY

opening the prison
of a three-headed bird
wiring bridges and mountain tunnels with explosives
a wedding party in front of the door
a small demon with an insect body
his face, peacefully radiant, remote from his torturers
the acrid smell of smoke filling the streets
hide indoors or get out of town
many arrived shaking and in tears
the top floors had collapsed
an ancient woman sweeping away the glass and debris
the shrub-covered hills at dusk, the evening star rising

FALLING FROM THE CLOUDS

like a swarm of insects
forces were extorting on a maximum scale
his body a broken egg shell
sitting alone at the bay window
sad red roofs with smoking chimneys
a mass of refugees mulling along
near the chemical factories
stray missile hits a large white drawbridge
under which a barge passes
an old man at the tiller
autumn trees in spring

A ROW OF HILLS,

blue in the evening mist
a few geese pecking at grass
a woman, hands calloused from hard work,
bends and picks up
a huge fire raging at the hospital
a deep crater blown out of one corner
a stray bomb between a school and a farmhouse
plunging down from the roof to the first floor
as firetrucks converged on
the smoking residential district
damaging railways and watermellons
watermains shooting like geysers
a small globe of earth placed carefully
upside down on a gallows
devoured by birds
flashes of catastrophes at sea
poisoned by the magician's wand
we seem to be imprisoned in some cage
these bleak winter days
lilac hues in the evening sky
like a field of young tomatoes, inexpressibly pure
dew appears in the grass
a sow with a litter of sucklings
in the twilight of that deep shadowy elm
how much light there is in darkness!

IN EARLIER ATTACKS

in earlier attacks yesterday
a flame shot out of a swan's beak
the expression of a sleeping baby
took refuge in a hole in the wall
thick black smoke filled the streets
closer to madness than to childhood
some bleeding from shrapnel wounds and others
from the glazed look of exhaustion
firefighters trapped inside
the weight of a fabric
while an old fool, fascinated by
the tricks of the illusionist,
does not see the blue demon
next to him playing a clarinet

VIEW FROM THE BARRED WINDOW

THE CLOUDS STAYED RED

long after the sun had set
over the massive explosions at the dental clinic,
injuring at least twenty seven memories
of plants and crustaceans like gnarled
trees with fantastic roots, while
the vast majority spent the night
in the rain, huddled along the road
cutting through fields of young green corn

THE ENTIRE SIDE WALL

was blown away, leaving
the TV studio with its two top floors
collapsed, a charred ruin, while an owl sat
on the withered branch of a hollow tree and
watched the river, as calm as a pond,
reflecting light of the gibbous moon

SUNSET BEHIND CLOUDS

the dreamer tripped over the long shadows
and fell into a well while the tide was
out, the water very low, but twisted hawthorne
bushes, their branches bent low to one
side by the wind, hampered rescue efforts, so
the doctors amputated his sense of compassion
to free him

CHUNKS OF CONCRETE

and broken glass
scatter over the ground; on the
horizon a strip of light, above it immense
dark clouds and slanting streaks of rain;
many trees lie about uprooted; a man
leans against the bridge rail, looks into
the dark water; birds begin to
sing at the first hint of dawn

THE RAVEN SPOKE ABOUT THE WAR
under conditions of anonymity

WHITE-CRESTED WAVES

as far as the eye can see
killed by paramilitaries
writers and schoolteachers, executed yesterday,
shed a golden light over the fields
a red brick house covered in ivy
blames the flight of wild ducks
while an elderly walled garden
blooming with lilacs and hawthorn
exhausted, in a state of shock,
sleeps in doorways and on sidewalks

BABBLING BROOKS ARE CARESSED BY

the spiral of violence
air raid sirens sound confessions of love
smooth thighs praise grim pictures
children stare out of windows, solemn and
gloomy,
egrets charbroiled beyond recognition
food medical supplies glide over pools of mother's
milk
anti-aircraft missile kissed beyond exhilaration
bodies of foxes crash into forgiveness

FIRST ROBIN OF SPRING

balancing funerals
lawyers pound earthworms for a sixth day
extremist groups rejoice under cottonwood trees
spreading sweet nothings like
propaganda on the dance floor
pearl necklaces surround thousand of refugees
as terrorists hurl passionate melodies
on violins engulfing
the buildings in a balmy afternoon

SPARROWS WHISPER ABOUT

the troubled province
hydrangea shake the city with strong
intimations
red peonies hit by surface-to-air missiles
carousels executed on Sunday
fantasies of crystal shot dead by police
ethnic hatred snapped the turtle's
endurance
gas masks dumped into
corn flowers
reliable sources reported

POUNDING THE SOUTHERN CITY

with strange haunting pictures
featherless birds launch new attacks against targets
dozens of rockets strike
the tree shaped like a hand
as a parade of naked men seated
on animals of every kind
fire missiles at three-fifteen a.m.
on the populated part of the city
helicopters and snipers augment
the usual security forces
with laws of color,
unutterably beautiful
while a grove of olive trees,
dark against the glimmering sky,
announces it is sending additional troops
and jets pummel a broad swath
across the disturbing tranquility of a woman

MISTAKEN IDENTITIES

THE HARROWING STENCH OF THE DEFENSE

The desperate face of hunger
pressed against the bars;
box tortoises writhe with
food poisoning; highway
potholes filled with murdered
squirrels; a seamstress slowly
dies of untreated
wounds; shredded paper
and commissioners' debris
covering the
tombstones at the refugee
camp stray bullets call the
faithful to prayer,
lawyers steal the medicine;
raw sewage floods the blanket
distribution center, soldiers
beat back the
widows pulling at the fence,
a grenade
rolls down the
playground slide.

Later that day the press conference
reeks of perfume,
the cameramen almost gagging.
Into the bank of microphones
the experts discuss

the intelligence data. The spokesman
carefully weighs
his words.
Reporters take scrupulous notes.
In all the stories filed not one mentions
the harrowing stench of the Defense
Secretary.

CAUGHT IN AN ENDLESS LOOP

the bristlecone pines entwine their roots
with the weeping willows
in the beauty parlor
the collaborator is shot dead
a carfull of double-crested cormorants
run over a landmine,
river rats frolic in the
choking clouds of prayer,
investment counselors pledge
revenge as a sacred duty,
a newly-wedded couple dreams of
bliss in the intensive care unit,
a licensed contractor orders the nuns
into the gutter, some with
newborn babies
in their arms.
Under cover of his emptiness,
the chief executive keeps spitting blood.
The surgeon carefully
slices the broken hearts.
Caught in an endless loop.

SCATTERED ABOUT THE VILLAGE WELL

Unexploded cluster bombs lay
scattered about the village well.
Nearby, a golden bouquet of mushrooms
sprouted from the sapwood rings
of a plum stump.
The entire marketplace was flattened
but what could we do?
Juniper berries scratched wounds
into our faces, a rufous
hummingbird alighted on a
topmost twig, a light
drizzle tattooed against the sagging
refugee tent while,
in a desolate and impregnable language,
the Pentagon denied all reports.
Beyond the shadow of the fires,
a mountain lion watched
the mud walls sinking slowly
back into the earth.

THE BOUNTY OF ACORNS

withered under a hail of artillery fire
while a raccoon family scampered
into the shadows where
dogs were pulling at what was left
of the full moon.
Groups of armed boys
roamed the dark streets,
looting the silence of crickets, while
burned-out tanks littered
the olive orchards, ten-foot craters
punctuated the libraries,
toddlers played hide-and-seek with
shell casings and land mines,
old women were afraid to go
to the bathroom and,
behind the rubble of red cirrus clouds,
flocks of band-tailed pigeons
gathered to mourn.

GREEN TREE FROGS SING

as rain drenches the gardens
and cemetaries. A salamander crosses
the road strewn with burning tires,
gas cannisters and shrapnel.
A fox sniffs cautiously
at the hair and feet of
the farmers and salesgirls piled
haphazardly in the ditch.
A swallowtail butterfly flutters
past the row of prisoners, hands wired
behind their backs.
The executions continue all day, while
bandits prowl the neighborhoods.
The soldiers look bored.
A small yellow beetle crawls
under dead leaves.
A scarlet tanager darts
to her nest, shrouded
in a sycamore, and
furtively feeds her chicks.

RED SQUIRRELS CHASE EACH OTHER

to a meadow where the postman,
wounded by stray bullets,
lies bleeding on top of a stand of
wooly yarrow, some
needlegrass and a few corn
flowers, which shake
with the thuds of the
seven-and-a-half ton
fireballs decorating the horizon.
Inside each fireball it is
the end of the world, while
a warbling vireo darts through
the wet aspen, viewing,
through its bird eyes,
the universe in every raindrop.

A SPLURGE OF SPIKED VERVAINS

Falling asleep to the sound of shelling
for three years,
the number of dead and wounded
unknown as moss
creeping along the underside
of an abandoned bunker,
writhing on a filthy matress
after walking barefoot
for seven hours, feet raw and bleeding,
charred trees left standing in a burnt forest,
yet home to badgers, mountain chicadees,
flying ants, thankful for exquisite memories
of almond tortes, morning kisses,
piles of autumn leaves,
a first teenage crush,
the x-rays showed projectiles lodged
near the base of their skulls, perhaps
topaz, mother-of-pearl
or strings of regret
pressing white-headed woodpeckers
into ponderosa pines:
clearly they had been executed.

Thus the Holy Month began and ended
in the Holy Land,
torn by maimed boys,
all books closed,

the blind physician drilling
haphazardly through legs,
adding wounds to faces,
as a red-crested nuthatch hopped down
a tombstone,
a splurge of spiked vervains
burst into clusters of tiny purple flowers,
and under a shady feldspar outcropping
a porcupine and a shy wolverine suddenly
fell in love.

SURROUNDED BY MIRRORS

the walls of your mind
become mirrors,
surrounding you in an ever-shrinking
infinity, surrounded by mirrors.

Cuddling a holiday morning
on a sumptuous pillow,
love redolent with delights,
beyond the reach of thistles, candles,
burning icons, frozen tears, vengeful
gods, corporate warlords, clotted
dreams, ragged small voices, the dim cell
depths, maimed girls waiting outside
the streets' eery silence,
surrounded by mirrors.

New buds burst on the magnolia while
others on the ground disintegrate,
the old oak woodpile, slowly rotting
into the earth alongside the ancient
stump, beneath the bark a world of
ants, beetles, worms, larvae, tiny eggs
taking back what's theirs,
filling your mouth with garnets,
luna moths,
precious moments of
forgetfulness, the ability to simplify,

starfish on sizzling beaches,
shady cottonwoods by warbling streams,
ladder-backed woodpeckers hammering
ponderosa
pines, milkweed seed-parachutes floating on
warm
breezes past rows of flattened shops
bribing the border guards with
the reek of burning tires
troops massing behind the shrine
newlyweds killed as they sleep
the mood of the desperate crowd running through
the streets swinging from hopeless resignation
to palpable defiance, you never know
until the explosion,
after and before darkness,
beneath the debris of unintended
targets, the unstoppable resurgence
of wildflowers,
beyond the reach,
surrounded by mirrors.

KEYS TO THE WAR ROOM

A LEAF TWIRLING

in a spider web,
pelicans dive headlong into the sea:
I wouldn't begrudge it to you, honey,
don't begrudge it to me.

Silent on a mountaintop
the cracks in an old wooden fence
dandelions in the school yard
a baby smiles at a cockroach
the guitar string breaks but the music streams on
she slowly lowers the jaguar mask
look! up in the sky!
the veins in a live oak leaf
the pains of betrayal
the discovery of electricity while
touching a knee
when I listen at least she speaks
if you know the truth why can't you sing it to me
Gorbachev watches fireflies at dusk
an old friend across the street
I brush your earlobe with the tip of my tongue
the hat you wore on your sixth birthday
what is washing a dish between a woman and
man
why are we all in the penitentiary
why do you smell different than you usually do
at 5 am I hear you turn the key

remember that feeling is everything
I wouldn’t begrudge it to you, honey,
don’t begrudge it to me.

SPLINTERS OF MIRROR

shattered on the floor
barbed wire screwed into your brain
the muffler bounces across the highway
the urinal is full
pitbulls only follow orders
why can't you help me
ease the pain
we must
we must become indigenous again

now the president paces in a teak-paneled room
the lawyer keeps his eye on the deck
a tenant writes a check he prays is good
a homeless prophet prays for Robin Hood
down by the bus stop a woman
decides to seize her own fate
beneath the concrete a seed quietly waits

why don't we just
ruminate together
your graduation picture still exists somewhere
between the lake and summer's end
you had a friend with frizzy hair
the scent of new-mown hay
I'll show you what is in my hand
if you come with me
to Camagüey

listen closely you can hear
the creek that once flowed
not far away
we must
we must become indigenous again

EARTHQUAKE UNDER THE OCEAN

the pain the rocks feel
the mind refuses anything at all
a hawk on the corner of your roof
the hand is only asking for a dime
in the eyes of a fleeing wolf

you climb a precarious trail beside a waterfall
risk your heart on the fall of a card
turn a corner on a moonless night
run a race you have no chance to win
touch a shoulder that's kept its feelings unspoken
kiss the palms of a woman who's worked
hard all her life
rush out to see the dawn
look into the eyes of a spirit unbroken

a flower choosing to open
take off your innermost disguise
roots delve bedrock deep
penetrate your heart in search of sleep
a potted plant wondering where to go
the river deciding which way to flow
six hummingbirds hover above your head
it's a law of the universe:

grow or die

MARRIES

bumblebee marries meteorite shower
midnight sky marries dandelion
icefloe marries redwood sprout
solarflare marries sealion
pile of autumn leaves marries
do you have a free night
you're kind of cute marries
sap of a pear tree
your lips are the full moon marries
you think you're always right
I hope you'll come back soon marries
you care more about him than me

hummingbird outside of your window marries
tear open your heart
accept the things you hate most marries
compassion for a shark
show me all your blemishes marries
why can't we be friends
you don't ever say you're sorry marries
nothing you can do will ever make amends
to prove your point you'd sit in a hole marries
it used to excite me to thrill you
I trust you as far as I can throw your soul marries
if you do that again I'll kill you
predictable but not reliable marries
our lives just aren't healing

it's worse than being alone marries
why are you so afraid of feeling

fingers touching rabbit marries
on your elbows and knees examine a clover
giving milk to a tabby cat marries
our lives are almost over
put on your oldest shoes marries
sitting on a bench in the park
whatever happened to your first doll marries
walk across a bridge in the dark
go ahead you know how marries
call me real soon
respect for the grass marries
dancing under the moon
grow old with friends marries
bellywop on a flexible flyer
forgive yourself for being human marries
hold the obsidian mirror up before the fire

THE DOLL OF A HOMELESS GIRL

Mannequin in the mirror
insane banker under the bed
Goddess in a straightjacket
tearing off her head
Let's get perspective on it:
hail bounces against the roof
a wedding march for the dead.

Disillusioned revolutionary
betray what you hold most dear
Bleeding woman needy man
do whatever pleases your fears
Let's get perspective on it:
nothing is ever whatever it appears.

River rat lame excuse
is a prophet with his hand in your pants
The president when no one follows orders
is a puma crouching on a branch
A sealion eyed by a shark
is the spirit of ceremonial dance
Let's get perspective on it:
morning dew
takes a desperate chance.

The dog of another world
is your lover causing you grief

That thing you clutch in your mind
holds communion with a false priest
Let’s get perspective on it:
the doll of a homeless girl
blows the conch shell on a deserted beach.

EYES VISUAL

spray foam on a breaker's crest
your lover trusting in you
the foreskin of an elk
Jupiter moves past Neptune
a pebble drops into Lake Michigan
those pants have a hole in the knee
the duck decides to walk backwards
polished nails fumble with a zipper
the stockmarket dives into a submerged obstacle
they extract ice needles from
the commander's favorite mirror
the governor's wife reveals her taste for
schnauzers
the chairman reaches for his hair die but picks up
the hot sauce instead
the autopsy reveals choking on lies
the election returns him over to the hyenas
Chaney on his death bed, the look on his face
when he realizes that
Lincoln is waiting for him on the Other Side

inner eyes outer sensual eyes
the scent of your lover in the morning
it's on the tip of your tongue
six reasons for not committing suicide yet
a young giraffe has her first period
you rise to the occasion

Mary, in her dream, discovers Harry's hand
inner outer eyes sensual
spiritual mental aural visual
you think with your open heart
your boss and landlord caught at the border
mother wades into the ocean
private ownership of land is hereby abolished
yourself in a sphere of flames

COLORWHEEL

red orange yellow green blue violet red
orange yellow green blue
twilight in a valley after a cold fall day
a fox peers out of a bramble
a patch of snapdragons sheltered by a dune
a parrot ruffles its neck feathers
the deepest spot in a tropical lagoon
sunset clouds over halfmoon bay

crimson stains on a stock certificate
dry leaves on a shallow grave
sallow skin of a starving child
gangrene in a prisoner's leg
the president's veins bulging with lies
as violet as a row of patriots rotting away

freckle on your lover's chin
tornado twisting fences aweigh
fiery lettering on a picket sign
you dig in a hillside of moist yellow clay
buds burst from a branch that looked dead
uniforms scatter at the break of day

FOR EVERY ACTION

the dry space beneath the waterfall
the sky in a green bathrobe
wood is the skeleton of the tree
yesterday we kissed the earth many times
snuggling your footsteps
climbing the scaffold remember your level
why aren't poets on live network tv?
because poetry is boring
you can't understand it
you never know what a poet might say
and crystal fragments shatter across the floor,
burying your heart down the deep twists of
tomorrow
while the U.S. army of North America
shoots uranium bullets while
an entire generation of young men
rot in filthy cells on low-level drug charges while
billions of tons of concrete are poured
into more prisons and guards, while
Coca Cola imports 500 metric tons of
coca leaves into the US each year for
"natural flavors," while
the CIA and international banks
run the cocaine trade and
while you lift a rotting log
in the deepest forest,
what will you find

under it?

An equal and opposite reaction.

NO MORE NATIONAL SCIENCE

the night of the quarry hides sobbing in brambles
while children writhe begging for absolution
no more

my love makes a vow she will bleed in the ocean
till statesmen's lies corrupt crescent moonrise
no more

father forbids the limp of the morning
fissioning scars
scalpel chastisment the stars
laundrymats whining for penance
doubtful saviors
meltdown reservoirs
classified hornet radar
laser ballistic biomass research
ulcering slash of greed in the hillside
writhing the stealth of assassins
in priests' smiles no more

no more
tv poisonous ashes of doom
no more
secret lab techno-cancer babble
no more
physics of mass deception
NO MORE NATIONAL SCIENCE

GREEN FLOWERS DRIZZLE DOWN

corn tassels swirling with copal incense,
pine seedwings blow from the golden conch,
scatter with each quaking house,
losing ourselves in these flowers
entering beyond where

dance wind beside the drum
waving your green plume fan
utter these stamens
our pain subsides
we whirl asleep in petals of dream
these holy buds bloom
the jade drum
the night sky passing through blossoms
falling pleasure as infinite as life
the aroma of wind on these lips
in the room of bracelets
the air redolent with pollen

VOWELS

in the control room demanding equal pay
vowels at the presidential dinner
carrying his head on a bamboo tray
vowels find you in the barn
and you tumble in the hay
very strange in the eyes of a bluejay

vowels by your lover's pillow
kissing a dimple on a fantasy
vowels beneath the bark of a sugar maple tree
vowels in the jump of a pregnant wallaby
vowels join a mariachi band outside of Cincinnati

vowels in a sunken city
watching the squids glide by
vowels on the old playground lawn
in the afterglow of a firefly
vowels at the court house dock
scrawling truth inside a thigh
vowels wonder if frogs feel guilty when they lie

vowels in the garden leaning on a magic hoe
vowels by the river bank
watching the pebbles flow
vowels on the marble stairs spraypainting the
word NO
vowels flying south upon a laughing crow

vowels atop a pyramid without one shoe
vowels down a tunnel to Timbuctu
vowels slips off her gloves and shows you her clue
vowels arm the people with meadow morning
dew
vowels sit by a waterfall
and gaze on through
and sometimes know why
because of
VOWELS

FORGET/REMEMBER

forget cats purr through their veins
forget this is a tunnel of glass
forget waving to mommy from the merry-go-round
forget entering the house of your inner nature
forget the second time you fell in love
forget handfuls of moist earth
forget no one won the war
forget it's only a mirror to your own light
forget to kiss your mother goodbye
forget this infinite eternity
forget you're not the first person to say that to me
forget to comfort your lover
forget you were given this gift to guard
forget it is a long way into the poem
forget the smell of autumn leaves
forget swearing you'd always remember that moment
forget when you had all the time in the world
forget new snow by early morning light
forget the clouds opening sweetly like knees
forget to be nice to the grass
forget this most perfect fire opal
forget the feet of the notyetborn
forget this does not belong to only you
forget accepting the pain
forget Rumsfeld will not be eligible for parole

forget the pigeons are listening
forget you are a direct descendant of
the first spark of life
forget to forgive the ones you don'tlove
forget to forgive the ones you love

remember
remember cats purr through their veins
remember this is a tunnel of glass
remember waving to mommy from
the merry-go-round
remember entering the house of your inner
nature
remember the second time you fell in love
remember handfuls of moist earth
remember no one won the war
remember it's only a mirror to your own light
remember to kiss your mother goodbye
remember this infinite eternity
remember you're not the first person to
say that to me
remember to comfort your lover
remember you were given this gift to guard
remember it is a long way into the poem
remember the smell of autumn leaves
remember swearing you'd always remember
that moment
remember when you had all the time in the world
remember new-snow by early morning light

remember the clouds opening sweetly like knees
remember to be nice to the grass
remember this most perfect fire opal
remember the feet of the notyetborn
remember this does not belong to only you
remember accepting the pain
remember Rumsfeld will not be eligible for parole
remember the pigeons are listening
remember you are a direct descendant of the first
spark of life
remember to forgive the ones you don'tlove
remember to forgive the ones you love

forget/remember

HOW DO WE KNOW OUR INALIENABLE RIGHTS?

What if self-evident truths
drop into the mind
as if from the skies,
beyond argument, reasoned
or unreasoned.

Do we know them
by reading the Declaration
of Independence?
Do we know
them by asking the lawyers?

And what about the Laws of Nature
and of Nature's God?
Do slaves need to debate
the right to rebel?

What if social justice is
inconvenient?
Or if workplace
democracy has been denied?

here
in the course of human events

SMILE

A lot of people in America
don't feel good.
How much of that is the social system?
how much is the human condition?
Does the Supreme Court have jurisdiction
to decide?

Does capitalism in fact
make people feel good?
This is ideological struggle!
And what about anarchism and Islam?
Let's get down to details!

Why bother
with a revolution at all
if it doesn't make people feel better?

Does competition and hoarding
make people
feel best,
or cooperation and sharing?

If a pleasure meter could record
how good people felt the world over,
how would Havana rate beside Las Vegas?
a sweatshop near Chesapeake Bay
beside a collective farm near Hue?

What if Minnesota scored
higher than Ukraine
but lower than the Basque region of Spain?

What if we consider the mountain meadows?
What if we ask the caribou?

Have you heard about the doctor who proposes
that we all practice smiling
a few times each day?
I checked it out and,
as soon as I got the hang of it,
I really felt much better.
Now I laugh a lot of the time.

When anybody asks me why,
I tell them it's because I
am a revolutionary.

"In our new society the people must
help each other.
If they do that, they'll feel better."
Mao Tse-Tung, 1944

HOMAGE TO GONZALO GUERRERO

HOMAGE TO GONZALO GUERRERO

In the year 8 Water,
the 11th tun in a 2 Ahau katún,
in the calendar of Castile the year 1511,
a small boat carrying seventeen shipwrecked
Spaniards washes up on the northern coast of
Lúumil Cutz U Lúumil Ceh,
the Land of Pheasant and Deer,
called by the Castillians, Yucatán.

These are the first Europeans to walk
in the land of the Maya, the Mayab.

Six tuns pass.
By the Maya year 1 Storm,
1517,
only two of the Europeans are still alive.
One, Gonzalo Guerrero, known as Warrior,
a seaman from Palos,
is now married to the daughter of
Ah Nachan Can, the Halach Uinic,
governor of the province of Chetumal.
Guerrero has become a Nacom, a lord of the
Serpent order.
The other shipwrecked Spaniard,
Jeronimo de Aguilar, known as Eagle,
has become a masehual, a common worker
attached to the lord of a small town near Chab Le.

Then in the year 1 Storm,
1517,
three ships in search of slaves
appear offshore from the coastal city Ecab.
From their decks the Spaniards can spy
the pyramids in the distance.
They declare the city
“Great Cairo,” and fancy themselves
the first Europeans to reach this land.
Ten huge Maya canoes with sails,
almost as long as the ships,
forty men in each, venture out, greet them
and invite them to shore.
The Spaniards wonder why the Mayas,
unlike most of the natives they encounter,
show no surprise or fear.
The Mayan delegates escort
them toward Ecab, then
slip into the brush.
The sky suddenly rains arrows.
A band of warriors attacks.
The strangers panic back to the shore,
thirteen wounded.

Unknown to
the Spaniards, among the Mayas
is the man Warrior.

The next year, the Spaniards return
for revenge, but again
are routed and flee.

Two more tuns pass.
Then, in the Maya year 3 Water,
1519,
called 1 Reed by the Aztec count,
Captain Hernán Cortés
leads a fleet of eleven ships, 110 sailors, 553
soldiers
and plenty of ammunition,
headed toward the great Aztec city
Tenochtitlán,
which glistens with gold,
or so they have heard.
Stopping at the island of Cozumel,
Cortés learns that on the mainland
two Spaniards are living with the Mayas.
He summons them,
sending as ransom strings of green beads.

Aguilar quickly reports to Cortés
and becomes his interpreter.
But Guerrero does not appear.
Cortés dispatches Aguilar back
to fetch him.

These are their very words,

recorded by one of the soldiers.

“Brother Aguilar,”
Guerrero Warrior replies,
“I am married, I have three children,
and am a chief and captain
in time of war. Go in God’s name!
My face is tattooed, my ears pierced.
What would those Spaniards think of me
if I went among them?
See how handsome these children are;
I beg you, give me some
of those green beads for them,
and I will say that my brothers
sent a gift from our country.”

His wife adds,
“Why has this slave come
to seduce my husband?
Be gone, speak no more.”

So Gonzalo Guerrero Warrior chooses
to remain a Maya.

Aguilar reports to Cortés, adding
that Guerrero advised the Mayas
to attack the Spaniards the year before,
and fought with them.

Cortés seethes,
“I wish I could get my hands on him!
It will never do to leave him here!”

But Cortés continues on to Tenochtitlán,
while in the Mayab eight years pass in peace.
Then in 11 Jaguar, 1527,
the army of strangers returns.

The Mayas of the eastern provinces
resist fiercely.
Pits are built to cripple horses,
barricades erected on approaches to towns,
food supplies cut off from the invaders.
The Mayas fight a guerrilla war,
leaving empty towns
to hollow victors in battles of attrition.
They are not bewildered
by the Spanish mind
and military tactics
as are so many other Native Nations.
The Mayas know how to deal
with the aggressors.

It took the Spaniards only
two years to defeat the mighty Aztecs,
only months to topple
the vast empire of Peru, but
a decade passes with no decisive battle, and

the Maya still hold the Mayab in their hands.

Gonzalo, Warrior,
you are the first European to understand and
respect Native culture enough to
marry into it,
make this your children's homeland, their people
your people, and defend them
in undying opposition to the rape and plunder.

Guerrero, Warrior,
I see you in the bushes by the river's edge
with a thousand comrades.
You are distinguished from them only
by your beard.
Your skin is tattooed into a book of glyphs,
painted black and red;
massive jade rings are in your earlobes,
a jewel embedded in your left nostril,
your long hair in four plaits coiled around your
neck.
A jaguar skin hangs from your shoulders
your head crowned with a great
fan of quetzal plumes, radiant green;
tucked into the belt of your breech-clout
is a dagger and a club.
In one hand is a small round shield,
in the other you clutch a thick trident
with three blades of sharpened shell.

Four Spanish ships in the channel lower boats
and their army quietly rows toward shore.
As they begin to disembark the air
is suddenly shattered with the throb of drums;
conch-shell trumpets wail, whistles shriek.
A storm of stones and arrows darkens the sky.
Out of nowhere your force leaps upon them
in hand-to hand combat.
You shout and slash, Gonzalo,
with your trident axe, the razor-sharp shells
tearing at their mark,
your quetzal plumes shaking and shining.

As you fall, a great serpent watches and
an iridescent green bird
flys wildly across the sun.

Guerrero, Warrior,
dead in battle by the Ulúa river, Honduras,
in the year 7 Jaguar, 1536,
a Spanish bullet in your head.
We honor you.

ABOUT THE AUTHOR

Author of twelve poetry collections, two novels, a memoir, and several histories. My translations of Inca, Maya, and Aztec poets are collected in *Ancient American Poets*. I was one of the founders of Indigenous Peoples Day in 1992, and have worked on the Berkeley powwow since then. Born in New York City in 1940, my family was a mixture of Romanian-Austrian Jew, Irish Catholic, English- Scottish Protestant, French and German. During the winters I grew up in Manhattan, and during the summers in New Jersey farm country without electricity or running water. My father was a post office worker, and my mother had been a dancer in Broadway musicals. I have a degree in Comparative Literature from New York City College, with a semester at the Sorbonne in Paris, France. I reside in Berkeley and have one daughter. I was a professional woodworker and cabinetmaker for over forty years at Heartwood Cooperative Woodshop. I served as chair of West Berkeley Artisans and Industrial Companies, and as a Berkeley planning commissioner. I was vice-president of PEN Oakland. My play *The Trial of Christopher Columbus* was produced by the Writers Theater in 2009. My transliterations from Pachacuti's Quechua formed the libretto for Tania León's *Ancient* (2009). I represented the USA at the World Poetry Festival in 2010 in Caracas, Venezuela. I have been a member of the Revolutionary Poets Brigade of San Francisco for many years, and an editor of their annual anthologies.

website:
https://johncurl.net/

ALSO BY JOHN CURL

Poetry:
America Beyond the Well (Homeward Press, 2025)
Memory of a Kiss (Homeward Press, 2025)
Rainbow Weather (Vagabond Books, 2022)
Yoga Sutras of Fidel Castro (Homeward Press, 2014)
Revolutionary Alchemy (Homeward Press, 2012)
Columbus in the Bay of Pigs (Inkworks /Homeward, 1991)
Decade (Mother's Hen, 1987)
Tidal News (Homeward Press, 1982)
Cosmic Athletics (Poetry For The People, 1980)
Ride the Wind (Poetry For The People, 1979)
Spring Ritual (Cloud House, 1978)
Insurrection/Resurrection (Working People's Artists, 1975)
Commu 1 (Gnosis Press, 1971)
Change/Tears (Drop City, 1967)

Poetry Translation:
Ancient American Poets (Bilingual Press, 2005).

Memoir:
Memories of Drop City (Homeward Press, 2008).

History:
Indigenous Peoples Day (IPD Books, 2017)
For All The People (PM Press, 2009, 2012)
History of Collectivity in the San Francisco Bay Area (Homeward Press, 1982)
History of Work Cooperation in America (Homeward Press, 1980).

Fiction:
The Outlaws of Maroon (Homeward Press, 2019)
The Coop Conspiracy (Homeward Press, 2014)

HOMEWARD

PRESS

www.ingramcontent.com/pod-product-compliance
Lightning Source LLC
LaVergne TN
LVHW020650100826
845148LV00012B/2421
* 9 7 8 1 7 3 3 5 7 7 5 6 4 *